On your own or with
Your siblings in tow,
Washing your hands
Is the way to go.

BABY SHARK knows
How fun it can be.
Let's wash our fins
Under the sea!

Wash your fins, doo doo doo doo doo doo.
Wash your fins, doo doo doo doo doo doo.

WASH YOUR FINS, BABY SHARK

Doo Doo Doo Doo Doo Doo

Art by John John Bajet

SCHOLASTIC

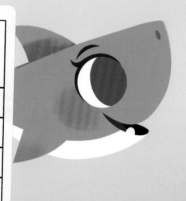

This edition published in the UK in 2020 by Scholastic Children's Books
Euston House, 24 Eversholt Street, London NW1 1DB
A division of Scholastic Ltd
www.scholastic.co.uk
London – New York – Toronto – Sydney – Auckland – Mexico City – New Delhi – Hong Kong

First published in 2020 by Cartwheel Books, an imprint of Scholastic Inc., U.S.A.
Copyright © Scholastic Inc., 2020
Adapted from the song, "Baby Shark".

ISBN 978 0702 30544 3

Wash your fins, doo doo doo doo doo doo.
WASH YOUR FINS!

Water on, doo doo doo doo doo doo.
Water on, doo doo doo doo doo doo doo.

Water on, doo doo doo doo doo doo. **WATER ON!**

Squirt the soap, doo doo doo doo doo doo.
Squirt the soap, doo doo doo doo doo doo.

Squirt the soap, doo doo doo doo doo doo.

SQUIRT THE SOAP!

Lather up, doo doo doo doo doo doo.
Lather up, doo doo doo doo doo doo.

Lather up, doo doo doo doo doo doo.
LATHER UP!

Scrub a dub, doo doo doo doo doo doo.
Scrub a dub, doo doo doo doo doo doo.

Scrub a dub, doo doo doo doo doo doo doo.
SCRUB A DUB!

Sing and wash, doo doo doo doo doo doo doo.
Sing and wash, doo doo doo doo doo doo doo.

Sing and wash, doo doo doo doo doo doo.
SING AND WASH!

Rinse those fins, doo doo doo doo doo doo.
Rinse those fins, doo doo doo doo doo doo.

Rinse those fins, doo doo doo doo doo doo.

RINSE THOSE FINS!

Dry them off, doo doo doo doo doo doo.
Dry them off, doo doo doo doo doo doo.

Dry them off, doo doo doo doo doo doo.
DRY THEM OFF!

Nice and clean, doo doo doo doo doo doo.
Nice and clean, doo doo doo doo doo doo.

Nice and clean, doo doo doo doo doo doo.
NICE AND CLEAN!

Teach your friends, doo doo doo doo doo doo.
Teach your friends, doo doo doo doo doo doo.
Teach your friends, doo doo doo doo doo doo.

TEACH YOUR FRIENDS!
WASH YOUR FINS, BABY SHARK!

BABY SHARK'S HANDWASHING TIPS!

Washing your hands keeps you and the people around you healthy!
Be sure to follow these tips:

WASH your hands often! Especially before eating food, after using the bathroom, and after you blow your nose, cough, or sneeze.

SCRUB your hands for at least twenty seconds. Need a timer? Sing three verses of Baby Shark!

LATHER your hands and wrists with soap, and don't forget to wash between your fingers and under your nails.

DRY your hands with a clean towel!

Washing your hands with soap and water is always best. But you can use an alcohol-based **HAND SANITISER** if soap and water aren't available!

Tips adapted from cdc.gov